Industrial Sales In America

Understanding and Planning For Sustainable Growth

RICHARD CRUZ

Richard_Cruz1@aol.com

INDUSTRIAL SALES IN AMERICA

Richard Cruz

Published by BooxAi

ISBN: 978-965-578-844-0

Content

Please Note: All opinions, perspectives, and documents contained within are solely those created by the author and are not intended to be representative of any specific individual, company, or organization.

Introduction

Every business seeks and desires year on year growth. However, sustaining growth in mature and evolving markets requires more than new products or simply placing more resources on the street.

Today, more than ever, it is critical that marketing and field selling organizations have a solid understanding of those behaviors that drive the decision making process, while executing business plans that identify and remove customer barriers early in the decision-making process. Equally important is management's responsibility to (1) Set realistic and meaningful expectations, (2) Create and maintain a positive and respectful work environment, while (3) Providing tools that dramatically decrease customer selling cycles and provide a greater understanding of the field forecast process and those important considerations, which are often overlooked in traditional forecasting.

Industrial Sales in America: Understanding And Planning For Sustainable Growth contains thirty-seven years of successful Sales, Marketing, International Market Development, and Business Management experience in Industrial Markets and reflects knowledge gained from those that I came to respect most in these areas including that from our most valued Distributor Partners.

My hope is that you find this an invaluable guide in moving your growth, consistently, beyond expectations.

Good Selling!

Personal History

- Education: Bachelor of Science…Bio-Chemistry
- Thirty-Seven Years With 3M Industrial Business
- Industrial Sales
- Domestic Marketing
- International Business Planning (Southeast Asia and Latin America)
- NAFTA (North American Free Trade Agreement) Market Development
- Area Business Manager (Industrial and Transportation Markets)

Corporate Recognition

- Professional Society Of Imagineers (Sales)
- International Esprit De Corps Award (Corporate)
- Professional Society Of Imagineers (Marketing)
- Corporate Nominee Marketing Excellence (Multiple)
- Area Business Manager Of The Year

General Business Perspectives

- **Wishing Harder Will Not Grow A Business.** However, a good plan, that is well executed, will.
- **In The Most Difficult Economic Conditions, There Are Always New Opportunities To Pursue** outside, and within, an existing customer base.
- **Business Cannot Be Grown Solely On The Backs Of Our Best People.** We must elevate the productivity of everyone in the middle if we are to achieve consistent and sustainable growth.
- **Our Best People Do The Right Things Instinctively.** Others must be taught. And, it is managements responsibility to provide meaningful tools to achieve that end.
- **Customers Do Business With Those They Respect And Trust.** Technology is only the starting point and an expectation by potential customers.
- **Credibility, Trust, And Loyalty Are Earned.** They are not entitlements.
- **Be Mindful That Being Right Does Not Always Mean You Will Win With Customers Or Within Your Organization.** Ultimately, customers and your management will make the final decision, and these must be respected.
- **Historically, Only 40 Percent Of Identified Opportunities Result In New Business.** This reality must be incorporated in the business planning process for individuals and organizations, alike.
- **There Are No Entitlements.** Customers, employment, and personal advancements must be earned.
- **Initial Success Earns Early Recognition And Promotions.** However, personal relationships and the respect of Senior Level Management, will ultimately define an individual's ability to access higher-level positions within a company.

- **Perception Is A Reality In The Eyes Of Many.** Therefore, situations should be managed with that understanding and sensitivity.
- **Customer Retention Should Be A Conscious And Integral Part Of Any Growth Strategy.** Managing attrition can significantly contribute to top line growth and should be done in concert with new customer acquisition efforts.
- **Uncompromising Integrity Must Be An Expectation Within Any Organization.** Without it, costs escalate and productivity declines.
- **Not All People Have The Same Skill Sets.** And this needs to be considered prior to assigning new responsibilities.
- **Market Share Gain In A "Me Too" Business Can Be Done Quickly And Profitably**. How?
  1. Be there first with solutions.
  2. Have more resources committed to identifying and qualifying new opportunities.
  3. Provide differentiated product options.
  4. Offer better terms.
  5. Provide local sources of supply.
  6. When justified, engage relevant corporate resources such as Laboratories, Research and Development, Marketing, Executive Management, etc. These, when used properly in support of customer priorities, lead to new business.
- **Aggressive Growth Planning** should include actions that represent not only traditional good business practices but also nontraditional activities that can accelerate the sales process and increase revenue while reinforcing invaluable relationships.

Examples:

1. Customer invitations to Corporate Headquarters
2. Insights into emerging technologies and test methods
3. Training on nonproduct-related subjects (Six Sigma, sales, etc.)
4. Personal Executive engagement when justified

Field Management Guidelines For Success

- **Hiring Good People Is The Best Insurance For Growth And Harmony Within An Organization** and can also be the most challenging. Education, high energy, high intellect, and motivation, combined with a history of success, are good starting places.
- **Generally, An Individual's Contributions Are More Important Than Their Annual Percentage Growth.** Percentage growth is only a moment in time and will be impacted (positively and negatively) by influences over which field selling organizations have little or no control. (Examples are declining local economies, business relocations/closures, lost contracts, and changes in statutes.) Ultimately, consistent growth will come to those where meaningful and measureable contributions are being made regularly, documented, and recognized.
- **There Is A Threshold To Sales Territory Size That Can Limit Forecast Attainment.** If a territory is too large (dollars), this can prove more of a plan for sales decline than growth. More customers require more maintenance, hence, allowing less time for new business development.
- **As Business Managers, It Is Critical To Know, Understand And Share Individual And Team Contributions.** Knowledge supports understanding of expectations while strengthening the commitment to excel.
- **Good Managers More Frequently Ask Others to Do Something Rather Than Tell Them.** Requests are always better received and imply respect for the individual.
- **Always Maintain A Positive And Respectful Workplace Environment.** This supports retention of your best people and enhance individual performance and continuous growth. Be mindful, the main reason people leave a company is because of dissatisfaction with their immediate supervisor.

- **Establish Clear And Achievable Expectations** particularly in these areas of performance: (1) New Customer Acquisitions, (2) Opportunity Identification and Documentation, (3) Distributor and End User Engagement, (4) Marketing Program Support, (5) Communications, (6) Customer Retention, (7) Meeting/Exceeding Forecast.
- **Recognition Is Paramount In Keeping A Stimulated And Productive Selling Organization.** Monitor progress and provide feedback on a regular basis.
- **Field Time With Representatives Is Essential** and should, generally, be considered an employee's time to share opportunities, to discuss issues, and to learn. Visitors should avoid excessive texting and cell phone conversations.
- **Managing Poor Performance Is Challenging And Time-Consuming.** The intent, by management, should always be to improve an individual's performance and make them a positive team contributor. At no time, however, should the supervisor care more than the employee, in accomplishing that objective.
- **Recognize That It Is Not Always The Responsibility Of Distributors To Grow A Manufacturer's Business, Nor Is It Always The Manufacturer's Responsibility To Grow A Distributor's Business.** Ultimately, that responsibility falls on their respective shoulders. However, when mutual and meaningful selection processes are followed by both parties and expectations are understood and agreed upon, solid relationships will ensue and result in the growth of both businesses.
- **Distribution Is Frequently Driven By Margin.** Distributor-selling organizations will often promote those products which are more profitable. That is, unless respect and trust exist between the Manufacturer and the Distributor-Selling Organization.
- **Time And Territory Management Cannot Be Overstated** and requires early training and continuous reinforcement.
- **Monthly Field Reports Can Be A Powerful Tool** but need to be managed wisely. It is a sound method for keeping an organization, and individual's, attention on priorities and enables the year-end performance appraisal process for both management and the field selling organization.
- **Do Not Burden Field Selling Organizations With Nonessential Activities** that detract from face-to-face contact with potential new customers or existing key accounts.

Field Sales
Planning For Growth

- **Be Fully Knowledgeable Of Products And Available Resources Within Your Organization.** This will dramatically shorten selling cycles and grow customer confidence.
- **Understand What Is Needed To Exceed Growth Expectations.** Considerations: 1) Current corporate forecast, (2) Effects of customer attrition on forecast attainment 3) Historical likelihood of closure on identified/open opportunities (40 percent), and (4) Recent closures. (See "Forecast Worksheet.")
- **Retain Existing Customers.** This reality dramatically contributes to meeting and exceeding sales forecasts. It is said that it costs nine times more to regain prior customers than to retain one.
- **Customers Do Business With Those They Respect And Trust.** These traits must be continually earned.
- **Manage Your Time Wisely!** A good starting place is (1) 65 percent of available time used pursuing new opportunities, (2) 25 percent maintaining existing customers, and (3) 10 percent managing administrative responsibilities. (Distribution should be considered a valued partner in points 1 and 2.)
- **Go Where The Money Is.** Prior to physical visits, have a good understanding of customer applications and potential product demand. Yours and the customer's time are valuable.
- **Early Identification Of Customer Priorities Is Critical!** This knowledge allows for early resource allocation, and assigned responsibilities within given time frames. All of which results in shortened sales cycles. (See "Sales Cycle Compression.")
- **Respond To Customer Requests Before Expected.** And give yourself a reason to return to affirm your reliability and their importance to you as a customer.

- **As Sales Professionals, We Are Generally With Customers To Provide One Of The Following:** (1) Improve the customer's product, (2) Reduce their material cost, (3) Increase productivity 4) Create safer working conditions for employees, or (5) to address environmental concerns. Efforts should always be directed at providing solutions to the customer's priorities.
- **If You Have A Question About A Customer's Business, Ask Them!** They will usually tell you.
- **The Higher Your Contacts Are Within An Organization, The Better Positioned You Are** to expand new opportunities and maintain existing business.
- **Decide, In Advance, If A Product Will Require A "Design" Specification, Or Be Used In The Manufacturing "Process."** This will help in directing your efforts to the proper decision maker and save valuable time. Examples: Process Engineer versus Design Engineer versus Marketing or Purchasing.
- **Do Not Abuse A Customer's Time With Non-Value-Added Visits.** Often, this can lead to highly restrictive access to facilities and decision makers within those organizations.
- **Today, Purchasing Relationships Will (and Do) Sustain Existing Customer Business.** This was not always the case. Today, however, most specifications contain "equivalency" clauses that allow for, and frequently require, purchasing to investigate less expensive alternatives resulting in either lost business or lower prices from their current suppliers.
- **Realize That Competition Is Always Present.** Not doing so will only leave business at risk.
- **Never Make Up Your Mind, In Advance, Of A Possible Customer Solution.** If it has merit, show it and let the customer make that decision. This often brings new insights and other application considerations into the conversation.
- **First Impressions Cannot Be Overstated.** Always present yourself professionally and be well prepared.
- **As A Sales Professional, You Do Not Have To Do It All Yourself.** Use all appropriate and necessary corporate resources to achieve objectives and accelerate the selling process. However, be mindful that responsibility for the customer, ultimately, remains with you.
- **Never Degrade A Competitor.** It only reflects on your character and that of your company.

- **There Are No Entitlements In The Private Sector.** Promotions, Raises, and Recognition are largely a personal responsibility and generally require good communication skills, and documented contributions in the areas of growth, teamwork, and support of marketing programs.
- **Maintaining Strong Distributor Relations And Communications Is Essential For Growth.** Distributors are often a primary source for new opportunities and play a key role in customer retention. Successful sales representatives have strong distributor relations.
- **Whenever Possible, Engage Company Executives With Your Most Important Clients And Opportunities.** This will increase your credibility and aides in accessing the decision makers within those organizations.
- **Having A Solid Understanding Of Customer Applications Is Critical.** And whenever possible, you should always align solutions using differentiated technologies.
- **Prior To Offering Deviated Pricing, Always Ask The Customer**, "If I am able to secure the target price you requested, will I earn your business?" Experience has shown that asking this simple question will get the business, far more often than not, when the target price is secured. On the other hand, if this question is not posed, your price will frequently be shared, and successfully used, to lower an existing competitor's price and allow them to retain the business.
- **Sources for New Customers.**
    - The Internet
    - Your Distributors
    - Colleagues
    - Trade Shows
    - Industrial Associations
    - Dun & Bradstreet SIC Listings (**S**tandard **I**ndustrial **C**odes)
- **More Is Learned By Listening than Speaking.**
- **Ask For The Order!** Orders may take many forms of (1) A request for a follow-up meeting to review test results, (2) Customer support for testing of another product option, (3) Agreement to a conference call with corporate technical resources, and of course, (4) A purchase order following a successful evaluation.

Distribution
Developing The Partnership

- **Distribution Should Be A Critical Component Of Any Growth Strategy.** When managed properly, distributors often become a primary source for new opportunities and a valued business partner in the marketplace.
- **Prior to (Suppliers) Establishing A New Distributor, It Is Important They Know, In Advance, What Role the Distributor Is Expected Play.** Be it (1) Providing a local source of supply to end user customers, (2) assisting in penetrating new markets, (3) Managing credit risk, (4) Offering more lenient terms of sale, (5) Becoming an extension of the supplier-selling organization, (6) Locally managing customer relationships, or (7) Identifying and qualifying new and competitive opportunities.
- **Margin Often Drives Distributor Behavior.** Be mindful that competitors frequently offer greater margins to distributors so as to insure product promotion by the distributor-selling organization. In this case, the distributor is often considered more the customer than the end user.
- **Distributors Respect Those Suppliers that They Believe Have A Strong Market Presence.** This understanding will assist suppliers in managing competitive threats and enhances distributor support on other business related subjects.
- **Direct (OEM/Manufacturer) Sales Should Be Considered A Last Resort In Markets Where Strong Channel Partners Are Active.** If not managed properly, these otherwise strong business partners can quickly become a supplier's largest competitor.
- **Local Expansion Of Distribution, By Suppliers, Is A Sensitive Subject Among Existing Distributor Partners** and should always be thoughtfully considered. Channel expansion will threaten relationships, reduce margins with existing distribution, and potentially encourage the introduction of less expensive competitive alternatives into those markets.

- **Manufacturers Should Continually Strive To Develop Programs that Encourage And Reward Distributor-Selling Organizations For Promoting Their Products.** These will help offset margins and other likely incentives offered by competitors.
- **Scheduled FieldWork With Distributor Representatives Cannot Be Overstated.** This activity supports relationships, personal credibility, and opportunity identification while enhancing distributor product knowledge.
- **Executive Visits To Distributor Headquarters Is Key In Establishing And Maintaining These Important Relationships.** Discussions on new opportunities and joint efforts often result here.
- **Product Training Should Always Engage Distributor Attendees And Be Scheduled Regularly.** This is the best time to discuss applications, opportunities, and schedule joint customer visits.
- **A Fast Way To Gain Distributor Loyalty** is to bring in new customer orders and assist with the development of new business within their existing customer base.
- **Unaccompanied Visits (By Suppliers) On Large Distributor Customers Is Sensitive** and best managed with an advanced phone call to the responsible distributor representative and informing them of your planned visit and objective. (Be mindful, they are commissioned representatives and their personal financial security often rests with these customers.)
- **Distributor Expectations Of Their Suppliers:** (1) Good margins on good products, (2) Regular product training, (3) Field sales and marketing support, (4) Customer leads, (5) Growth incentives, (6) Product availability, (7) Supplier management engagement, and (8) Product exclusivity (an unusual occurrence).
- **Suppliers Should Never "Knowingly" Make A Joint (Distributor) Visit On Customers Who Are Currently Purchasing Their Products From Another Distributor.** When new applications are identified by a second distributor, then, it is best for the supplier to (1) Make the visit on their own, (2) inform the customer that they are making this visit on behalf of the second distributor, and (3) Following the visit, contact the second distributor, and inform them of your progress on the new application.

Growth Acceleration Tools

Field Forecast Worksheet

The "Field Forecast Worksheet" is a one-page spreadsheet, created to help selling organizations better understand the following relationships in achieving and exceeding business forecasts:

1. Attrition (6 Percent) can vary upon Geography/Industry and the Economy

2. Target Account Acquisition (only 40% success factor awarded)

3. Recent Closures (100 percent Valuation)

Yearly Business Plan/Forecast (Template)

Representative Name: ______________________

Last Year Sales	$0	**PROJECTED ATTAINMENT**	
Yearly Forecast %:	8.0%	This Year $ Forecast:	$0
Dollar Forecast	$0	40% Targets + Closures:	$0
6% Loss Factor (Attrition)	$0	$ Needed TY w/ 6% Attrition	%
Diff. Last Year vs. This Year:	$0	$ Needed TY w/o Attrition	%
Pot. $ Needed For TY Attainment	$0	Current YTD Sales Growth	%

Current Year Target Accounts

Account Name	Products	$	Comments
	Total =	$0	
	Total =	$0	
	@ 40% Success =	$0	

Prior Year Closures [Q3/Q4]

Account Name	Products	$	Comments
		0	
	Total Dollars =	$0	

*Fill In Shaded Areas Only

Yearly Business Plan/Forecast (Example)

Representative Name: __ **John D.**______________________

Last Year Sales	$2,500,000
Yearly Forecast %	8.0%
Dollar Forecast	$2,700,000
Attrition (6% Loss Factor)	$150,000
Difference Last Year versus This Year	$200,000
Pot. $ Needed For TY Attainment	$350,000

PROJECTED ATTAINMENT	
This Year dollar forecast	$2,700,000
40% Targets and Closures	$259,000
$ Needed TY w/ 6% Attrition	$2,850,000
$ Needed TY w/o 6% Attrition	$2,700,000
Current YTD $ Sales Growth	**6.7%**

Current Year Target Accounts

Account Name	**Products**	**$**	**Comments**
Majestic Products	Product A	100,000	Evaluating Equipment
Los Angeles Series Corp	Product B	50,000	Need Eng. Approval
Excellent Systems	Product C	120,000	Budget Issues Resolved
San Diego Golf	Product D	10,000	Testing
Value Signage	Product E	25,000	Competitor 15% Less
	Total =	$305,000	
	Total =	$305,000	
	At 40% Success =	$122,000	

Prior Year Closures [Q3/Q4]

Account Name	**Products**	**$**	**Comments**
Vintage Wood Products	Product A	80,000	10% Growth Expected
Window World	Product B	30,000	New Business
Solar Time Products	Product C	22,000	Conducting Environ. Tests
Marina Storage	Product D	5,000	Requesting Lower Price
	Total Dollars =	$137,000	

*Fill In Shaded Areas Only.

End-User Maturity Mix

The End-User Maturity Mix Spreadsheet is a tool intended to measure an individual's productivity, both long and short term. What is revealed here is whether or not the individual (or team) is surviving on an aging customer base and if more attention is needed in the area of new customer development.

End-User Maturity Mix (Template)

Account Name	$ Volume	Years as Customer	Product Group
Total $ Reported:	**$0**		
		Total $	**% of LY Total $**
Accounts @ 5 yrs:			
Accounts @ 4 yrs:			
Accounts @ 3 yrs:			
Accounts @ 2 yrs:			
Accounts @ 1 yr:			
Total Accounts Reported:	0	$0	
Total Dollars Reported:		**$0**	
Last Year Total Compensation Dollars:		**$0**	
% Reported of Total:			
*Fill In Shaded Areas Only.			

End-User Maturity Mix (Example)

Account Name	$ Volume	Years as Customer	Product Group
Flight lines	400,000	5	
Uptown Graphics	175,000	4	
Marine Time	100,00	4	
Escalation Graphics	80,000	3	
Cross Construction	65,000	1	
SeaWorthy Designs	40,000	5	
Cherry Wood Inc.	25,000	5	
Sunny Land Planning	25,000	5	
Tomorrows News	20,000	4	
Sunset Bedrooms	18,000	4	
Timeless Frames	16,000	2	
California Covers	15,000	3	
Closet Manufacturing	15,000	3	
Solar Inc.	12,000	2	
Everything Metal	12,000	1	
OK Distributors	10,000	1	
Letter Graphics	10,000	2	
Contempory Arts, Inc.	10,000	3	
Instant Solutions	10,000	1	
Nevermind Products	8,000	1	
Odum Electronics	7,000	3	
Alfa Dimensions	6,000	2	
Tahiti Fashions	5,000	2	
Base Effects	5,000	2	
Motor Fabrication	5,000	1	
Total $ Reported:	**$1,094,000**		
		Total $	**% of LY Total $**
Accounts at 5 years	4	$490,000	19.6%
Accounts at 4 years	4	$313,000	12.5%
Accounts at 3 years	5	$127,000	5.1%
Accounts at 2 years	5	$54,000	2.2%
Accounts at 1 year	6	$110,000	4.4%
Total Accounts Reported:	24	$1,094,000	
Total Dollars Reported		**$1,094,000**	
Last Year Total Compensation Dollars		**$2,500,000**	
Percentage Reported of Total		**43.8%**	
*Fill In Shaded Areas Only.			

Sales Cycle Compression

"Sales Cycle Compression" is a process designed to accelerate target account closure rates. Information captured in the document assists the Representative (and Management) in quickly identifying customer barriers by answering a series of questions relating to a given opportunity. This process dramatically shortens the selling cycle while increasing sales effectiveness and closure rates at end users.

Benefits Include:

- Faster Closures,
- Clear Direction for Seasoned Representatives,
- Sharper Learning Curves for New Representatives,
- More Efficient and Productive Selling Organizations,
- Utilizing Business Management Expertise for Coaching,
- All Resulting in "**Accelerated Growth**"!

Target Account Acceleration Plan (Template)

Situational Analysis: (Most critical component of the Action Plan. Barriers and opportunities are identified here. Good documentation of facts relating to customer is essential. Highlight barriers in Red.)

Customer Name:
Dollar Potential:

- ⑨ How long has this been a target account?
- ⑨ What is the application?
- ⑨ Is this a cost reduction, product improvement or safety related?
- ⑨ Was this customer initiated?
- ⑨ Is this a customer priority?
- ⑨ Any Federal, State or Local regulations that must be met?
- ⑨ Who is our primary contact?
- ⑨ Who is the final decision maker?
- ⑨ What is your relationship with customer (business, personal)?
- ⑨ How is our company perceived?
- ⑨ Customer identified needs, wants, concerns?
- ⑨ Has our credibility been established?
- ⑨ What are the product needs/characteristics?
- ⑨ Competitive weakness/strengths?
- ⑨ What are our strengths/weaknesses?
- ⑨ Any previous evaluations/results?
- ⑨ Variable costs/issues? (energy, disposal, documentation)
- ⑨ Anticipated customer needs?
- ⑨ Cost analysis completed? Agreement?
- ⑨ Unit price of competitive material?
- ⑨ What is their cost of Quality? (waste, returns, rework)
- ⑨ Are there any budget considerations?
- ⑨ Other issues?

Objectives: Primary function of these objectives is to remove all barriers identified in the situational analysis. Keep objectives specific to a barrier.
(Do not identify individual responsibilities or time frames at this time. These will be captured in "Strategies")

1.
2.
3.
4.
5.
6.

Strategies: (These are the actions that will be taken against each objective described above. Specifically, Who will do What and by When.)

1.
2.
3.
4.
5.
6.

Results:

Target Account Acceleration Plan (Example)

Situational Analysis: Most critical component of the Action Plan. Barriers and opportunities are identified here. Good documentation of facts relating to customer is essential. Highlight barriers in *Red.*

Customer Name: Tier I Supplier and OEM
Dollar Potential: $100,000+

- How long has this been a target account? 2 years
- What is the application? Double coated tape laminated to P/E foam. (Part size 5" x 7").
- Is this a cost reduction, product improvement, or safety related? Cost reduction
- Is this customer initiated? No. We came to them.
- Is this a customer priority? No. Current product works.
- Any Federal, State, or Local regulations that must be met? No
- Who is our primary contact? Owner of Tier I supply company
- Who is the final decision maker? Tier I owner and OEM process engineering
- What is your relationship with customer (business or personal)? Strictly Business
- How is our company perceived? We offer good products, but we are more expensive
- Customer identified needs, wants, and concerns? Product must work and be much less expensive
- Has our credibility been established?
- What are the product needs/characteristics? Tape must hold the foam to metal piece which is then shipped to OEM for final assembly of finished parts. The foam then acts as a noise damper (sandwiched) between two metal parts
- Competitive weakness/strengths? None known to exist
- Our strengths/weaknesses? Price is too high
- Any previous evaluations/results? Yes. Products worked, but again, pricing was an issue
- Variable costs/issues (such as energy, disposal, documentation)? None
- Anticipated customer needs? Must have reliable source of supply.
- Cost analysis completed? Agreement by customer? No
- Unit price of competitive alternative? $ 4.50/sq.mtr. (factory cost)
- What is their cost of Quality? (waste, returns, rework)? None that we are aware of
- Are there any budget considerations? Yes…alternative product must work and be less expensive.
- Other issues?

Objectives: Primary function of these objectives is to remove all barriers identified in the situational analysis. Keep objectives specific to a barrier.

(Individual responsibilities will be identified in the next section…"Strategies.")

1. This change must be made a priority to the customer, which can only be achieved by providing a much less costly alternative that works.
2. Become more knowledgeable of end-user application. (Visit the Manufacturer's plant…view and fully understand the application.)
3. Get our Senior Management engaged. Offer lunch/dinner with Tier I and End-User preceding any testing, if possible.
4. Work with laboratory and marketing to identify suitable products for testing and arrange target date for evaluation at End-User.
5. Assuming successful completion of testing/evaluation, have a multi-year agreement prepared for signature by the Tier I supplier.

Strategies: These are the actions that will be taken against each objective described above, specifically, Who will do What and by When…

1. Sales Representative to arrange visit (thru Tier I supplier) to End-User assembly plant to review actual application. (This week…2/5)
2. Sales Representative to discuss application with Lab and Marketing, following plant visit and share observations and assist in selection of alternatives for testing. (2/6)
3. Laboratory to conduct initial internal tests and provide results to Sales Representative and offer product suggestions for evaluation by Tier I supplier. (by 2/20)
4. Representative to arrange management visit to End-User plant to discuss product options and establish specific test dates…invite Tier supplier, and End-User to lunch. (2/23)
5. Sales Representative to complete testing at Tier I supplier by 3/10 and at Manufacturer's assembly plant by 3/20.
6. Upon completion of a "successful" evaluation, Sales and Marketing to prepare Value Analysis and present 24-36 month extended agreement, guaranteeing the price to the Tier I Supplier. (3/28)

Results: A New Customer!

1. Visit to End-User plant confirmed that double coated tape need only adhere the foam to metal, long enough (and until) mechanical attachment at the OEM during final assembly.
2. Hence, our best 3/4" double coated tape worked very well and, ultimately, would be substituted for the competitive 5" wide d/c tape holding the foam to the metal… resulting in substantial savings to the Tier Supplier and the End-User.
3. A multi-year pricing agreement has been signed for (24 months). Full profitability was achieved…and a price deviation was not needed.

Monthly Field Reports

Monthly Field Reports can be an invaluable tool not only for Management, but more importantly, for the Field Representatives themselves, in keeping their attention on (and maintaining) good documentation of those activities deemed priorities by management.

Monthly Field Report (Template)

Monthly Field Report

Name	Month	

Target Account Progress (List all by customer name, potential dollars, and status)
Red-Flag Items (Business In Jeopardy)
Competitive Activity (End User and Distributor)
New Business
Distributor Programs
Seminars/Customer Surveys
Visitors: Marketing, Technical Service, and Management (include visitor dates)
Other

Monthly Field Report (Example)

Name:	John D.	**Month:**	July

Target Account Progress (list all by customer name, potential dollars and status):
• Blue Eagle…$150,000. Arranging plant visit by Laboratory • AAA Furniture and Hardware…$100,000. Product did not work. Need alternative • Banter Signs…$100,000….Closed. First order enter for 1 pallet • Taylor Concrete…$75,000. Closed. Signed Extended Agreement. $10,000 order entered w/Dist. • Mission Plastics…$90,000. Laboratory testing options. Should have cust. samples by early Aug.
Red Flag Items (business in jeopardy):
• US Ship….Out of stock and no local inventory. They are seeking competitive alternative ($50K) • Shurewind Scales…New buyer seeking lower cost alternatives ($75K)
Competitive Activity (end user and distributor):
• (See Above)
New Business:
• Garden Fixtures…$10,000. • Military Distributor…$20,000. • Halogenics...$5,000. • Canopy Graphics…$15,000.
Distributor Programs:
• 7/12 Amber Dist.….Equipment Product Training • 7/13 Alignment Supply…Sales Training.

Seminars/Surveys and Misc.:
• Naval Supply Depot….Industrial Products Seminar
Converter Activity:
• Two visits (7/25-7/28) made to Auto Manufacturer to view die-cut results…Order expected next wk.
Visitors: Marketing/Technical Service/Management etc. (include all visitors/dates since Sept.)
• 7/12 Mike Smith (lab)….Follow-up on testing with marine manufacturer. • 7/15 Leslie Adams (Mktg)…Industrial customer visits • 7/27 Bob Field (Div. GM)…Visits to key accounts/Distribution/new opportunities

Note: Above information are examples only and company names are fictitious.

Common Market Terminology

- **Channel**: Frequently refers to the means by which product will introduced, sold and delivered to a customer.
- **SOS: S**ource **O**f **S**upply
- **LNSP: L**ow **N**et **S**elling **P**rice (Factory Cost / Percent Factory Cost = LNSP)
- **OEM: O**riginal **E**quipment **M**anufacturer
- **Distributor Margin:** (Selling Price-Cost)/Selling Price
- **Local Content:** The dollar value (as a percent) of local materials and/or labor, contained in finished products (common terminology in International Manufacturing and Marketing).
- **Landed Cost Factor:** The added cost to have product delivered to another country.
- **Design Applications:** Those applications where a product is identified in a written specification and generally becomes a part of the finished product. Primary contacts would be Design Engineering and Marketing.
- **Process Applications.** Products are only used in the production process and seldom become a part of the finished goods. In this case, specifications are not always required. The primary decision makers in this case would be a Process Engineer, Production Manager, and Purchasing, since these decisions often affect production costs, for which they often have responsibility.
- **Direct Sales:** Products are sold directly to End-Users by the manufacturer. (There is little to no distributor involvement.)

- **Variable Compensation:** Refers to compensation beyond salary alone. They frequently include rewards for: 1) Individual or team growth versus forecast; 2) Trial orders; 3) New customers; 4) Distributor presentations; 5) New product sales and; 6) Customer contracts, etc.
- **Drop-Shipments:** Distributor orders are entered with the Manufacturer who then ships the product directly to the Distributor's customer. Customer billing remains with the Distributor.
- **Tier I/Tier II Suppliers:** Tier I Suppliers provide materials directly to the manufacture. Tier II Suppliers provide materials to Tier I Suppliers.
- **Manufacturer's Representatives:** Private companies and individuals that contract with Manufacturers to sell their products. Generally, day-to-day sales costs are absorbed by the manufacturer's and their compensation is then based solely on actual sales.
- **JIT: J**ust **I**n **T**ime
- **KBI: K**ey **B**uying **I**nfluence
- **FAB: F**eatures, **A**dvantages, and **B**enefits
- **Deviated Pricing:** Non-published pricing usually requiring Marketer's approval.
- **Factory Cost:** Generally, comprised of: a) research and development; b) Raw materials; c) Labor; d) Sales and Marketing costs and; e) Freight.
- **Sales Cost:** Frequently defined as a percentage of an Operating Units total cost of getting their product to market. This will vary from company to company as well as from product to product.
- **End Users:** Those companies that actually use your product in their pro-duction process.
- **Direct Reports:** Those employees who report to a Supervisor.
- **OUS/EU/SEA/LA: O**utside the **U**nited **S**tates, **E**uropean **U**nion, **S**outh **E**ast **A**sia, and **L**atin **A**merica

Other Market Terminology

Notes

www.ingramcontent.com/pod-product-compliance
Lightning Source LLC
LaVergne TN
LVHW071213160826
845679LV00003B/818

9789655788440